The stories at this level

There are very few words in these stories, pictures as in the text. The simple text and the characters who live in West Street. Y remember the words very quickly, altho them out letter by letter. This is fine: recognising and remembering words are very important skills in early reading.

Before you start reading with your children, read the story and activities first yourself, so that you become familiar with the text and the best way to give it expression and emphasis when reading it aloud.

Always sit comfortably with your child, so that both of you can see the book easily.

Read the story to your child, making it sound as interesting as possible. Add comments on the story and the pictures if you wish. Encourage your child to participate actively in the reading, to turn over the pages and to become involved in the story and characters. Even though children can't read, they enjoy guessing what is going to happen from the pictures, and talking about the emotions of the story.

This may be enough for one sitting, but don't give your child the idea that the book is finished with. Encourage your child to take the book away and to look through it alone, to find any bits that either of you particularly enjoyed.

Next time you look at the book with your child, suggest "Let's read the story together. You join in with me." The text in the speech bubbles is often the same as the text at the bottom of the page, so one of you can read the text in the bubbles, and one can read the text at the bottom of the page. This time follow the words with your finger under them as you read. Don't stop to repeat words; keep the interest up and the story line flowing along.

Now ask your child, "Do you want to read the story to me this time?" If your child would like to do this, join in where necessary if help is needed. The timing of this stage will depend on your child's readiness

1

to take over. Do not rush! Try to avoid the idea that reading is a great race where you are always urging children on to harder and harder text.

The activities at this level

The activities at the back of the book need not be completed at once. They are not a test, but will help your child to remember the words and stories and to develop further the skills required for becoming a fluent reader.

The activities are often divided into three parts.

One part is designed to encourage you both to talk about the stories, to predict what will happen and to recall the main events of the story.

One part encourages children to look back through the book to find general or specific things in the text or the pictures. Your child learns to begin to look at the text itself, and to recognise some individual words and letters. Don't press on with these activities too quickly; your child may need to wait a bit before tackling them. Children's general understanding of a story often comes before their ability to make distinctions between individual words and letters.

One part suggests drawing or writing activities which will help your children feel they are contributing actively to the story in the book.

When you and your child have finished all the activities, read the story together again before you move on to another book. Your child should now feel secure with it and enjoy being able to read the story to you.

Silly dog

by Helen Arnold

Illustrated by Tony Kenyon

A Piccolo Original
In association with Macmillan Education

Here, Dennis.

Fetch it.

Fetch it, Dennis.

Good dog.

Fetch it.

Silly dog.

Hello, Mr Singh.

Fetch it, Dennis.

Hello, Mrs Rocco.

Here, Dennis.

Come here, Dennis.

Dennis!

Looking at the pictures and words with your children

1. Dennis was a silly dog, wasn't he? Can you find all the times the word silly comes in the story? Point to them. How many times did you find it?

Dennis was good too. Can you find the word good in the story? Point to it.

Do you think Dennis was silly or good? Why?

2. Liz said 'Hello' to other people in the story. How many times can you find the word Hello Point to them. Who did Liz say 'Hello' to?

3. Liz and Len are trying to train Dennis.
What do they say to Dennis when they want him to get the ball?

Does Dennis obey?

What did Dennis do the first time Len threw the ball?

What did Dennis do the first time Liz threw the ball?

Things for your child to do

1. Draw Dennis and copy his name Dennis under the picture. (Trace the name for a young child.)

Draw the cat in the tree and write cat underneath.

2. Say to your child: "I'll tell you the story now. It won't be quite the same as the story in the book. When I stop, you guess what word I am going to say next."

Len and Liz were in the garden with Dennis. Len threw a _____ for Dennis. Dennis was feeling lazy. He didn't want to _____ the ball. Then Liz threw the ball. Dennis began to run after it, but then he saw a _____. He chased the cat up a _____. Then Dennis saw Mr _____ at the gate. Liz said _____ to Mr Singh and Mr Singh gave her back the ball. Liz threw the ball again, but this time Dennis saw. Mrs _____ coming along the road. Then Dennis saw Tamla playing with a ball in her _____. Dennis decided he wanted to play with Tamla so he _____ over the fence. He fetched Tamla's ball and brought it _____ to her.

3. Look at the last page of the story. Ask your children what they think might happen next. Help them to make up a story to follow on from this last page.

31

These activities and skills:	will help your children to:
Looking and remembering	hold a story in their heads, retell it in their own words.
Listening, being able to tell the difference between sounds	remember sounds in words and link spoken words with the words they see in print.
Naming things and using different words to explain or retell events	recognise different words in print, build their vocabulary and guess at the meaning of words.
Matching, seeing patterns, similarities and differences	recognise letters, see patterns within words, use the patterns to read 'new' words and split long words into syllables.
Knowing the grammatical patterns of spoken language	guess the word-order in reading.
Anticipating what is likely to happen next in a story	guess what the next sentence or event is likely to be about.
Colouring, getting control of pencils and pens, copying and spelling	produce their own writing, which will help them to understand the way English is written.
Understanding new experiences by linking them to what they already know	read with understanding and think about what they have read.
Understanding their own feelings and those of others	enjoy and respond to stories and identify with the characters.

First published 1988 by Pan Books Ltd, Cavaye Place, London SW10 9PG

9 8 7 6 5 4 3 2 1

Editorial consultant: Donna Bailey

© Pan Books Ltd and Macmillan Publishers Ltd 1988. Text © Helen Arnold 1988

British Library Cataloguing in Publication Data
Arnold, Helen
Silly dog. — (Read together. Level 1).
I. Title   II. Series
428.6   PE1119
ISBN 0–330–30212–4

Printed in Hong Kong

This book is sold subject to the condition that it shall not, by way of trade or otherwise be lent, re-sold, hired out or otherwise circulated without the publisher's prior consent in any form of binding or cover other than that in which it is published and without a similar condition including this condition being imposed on the subsequent purchaser

Whilst the advice and information in this book are believed to be true and accurate at the time of going to press, neither the author nor the publisher can accept any legal responsibility or liability for any errors or omissions that may be made